J. N. G. RITCHIE

D1189253

BROCHS OF SCOTLAND

Second edition

SHIRE ARCHAEOLOGY

2

Cover photographs
Three Scottish brochs (photographs by the author):
(top left) Dun Troddan, Glenelg, Lochalsh, Highland;
(top right) Mousa, Shetland;
(bottom) Gurness, Mainland Orkney.

British Library Cataloguing in Publication Data:
Ritchie, Graham, 1942–
Brochs of Scotland. – (Shire archaeology; 53).
1. Brochs – Scotland.
I. Title
936.1'1
ISBN 0 7478 0389 7

Published by
SHIRE PUBLICATIONS LTD
Cromwell House, Church Street, Princes Risborough,
Buckinghamshire HP27 9AA, UK.

Series Editor: James Dyer.

ISBN 0 7478 0389 7.

First published 1988; second edition 1998.

Printed in Great Britain by
CIT Printing Services Ltd, Press Buildings,
Merlins Bridge, Haverfordwest, Pembrokeshire SA61 1XF.

Contents

Acknowledgements

I am grateful to Mr James Dyer, Dr Anna Ritchie, Mr J. B. Stevenson and Dr Carol Swanson for many helpful suggestions which have been incorporated in the text. The contribution of Dr E. W. MacKie to broch studies and excavation will be immediately apparent. The assistance of Dr D. V. Clarke and Mr I. Scott, Royal Museum of Scotland, is gratefully acknowledged.

The following institutions and individuals have kindly given permission to reproduce illustrations: Professor D. W. Harding (figure 5); Mr John Hedges (figure 18); Historic Scotland (figures 4 and 6); Mrs Betty Naggar (figure 19); Orkney Library, Kirkwall (figure 9); Royal Commission on the Ancient and Historical Monuments of Scotland (figures 2, 14, 15, 17, 20, 21, 22, 23, 24, 25, 26, 27 and 28; and Royal Museum of Scotland (figures 7, 8, 10, 11 and 13). The plans (figures 3, 12 and 16) have been prepared by Mr I. G. Scott.

List of illustrations

1
Introduction

The broch towers of iron age Scotland are a unique architectural invention, their distinctive form and often majestic location capturing the imagination of tourists and archaeologists, as well as of those who live daily in their shadow. The visitor to the Highlands and Western Isles of Scotland is often puzzled by the names on the Ordnance Survey maps; brochs, duns, wheel-houses are so different from the forts and hut-circles of downland England. This volume seeks to explain the architectural peculiarities of brochs and to explore some of the notions about their origins.

Brochs are circular drystone fortifications, densely concentrated in the west and north of Scotland in Skye, Caithness, Orkney and Shetland, but occurring sporadically further south as well (figure 1). Most were probably built during the first century BC and the first century AD (although the dating evidence is, at best, equivocal), but the idea of the broch seems to have been developing since about 600 BC, and fully fledged brochs remained in use until at least about AD 200. Even after that date their shells remained the focus for settlements well into the Early Historic period (about AD 400-1000).

Brochs were among the first Scottish archaeological sites to attract the attention of eighteenth-century travellers such as Pennant and the fascination of dramatic situations like that of the Broch of Borwick in Orkney has not lessened. What is their origin? When and by whom were brochs built? The wide range of possible answers to such questions is a measure of the uncertainty of much of the chronological evidence (how we interpret the objects and the radiocarbon dates) and an indication of the difficulty of working out the sequence of stone-built structures that have been altered and reconstructed in the course of their history. The literature on brochs is so extensive and there have been so many conflicting views in the past that only a selection of the most important points is reviewed here.

Brochs are exciting to visit because of the sophistication of many of their structural details; because they are often comparatively well preserved, we can readily imagine the way of life of the important farmers who built them. They are of interest too for the many theories that have been put forward about why they were erected and in which part of northern and western Scotland

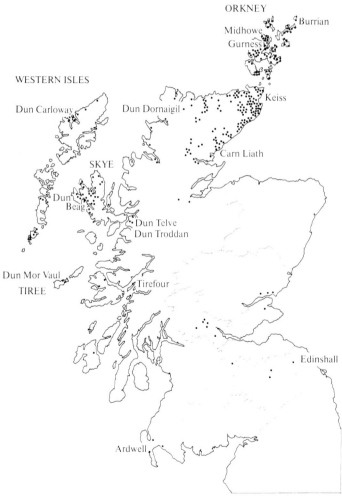

1. Distribution of brochs in Scotland, showing the location of the major sites mentioned in the text.

broch-building first developed. There is also the question whether the invention was a purely local one, or whether the arrival of new groups of people, either as refugees or as conquering chieftains, provided the impetus for their building.

2. Dun Telve, Glenelg, Lochalsh, Highland. This is one of the earliest illustrations of a broch and was drawn by Moses Griffith in 1772.

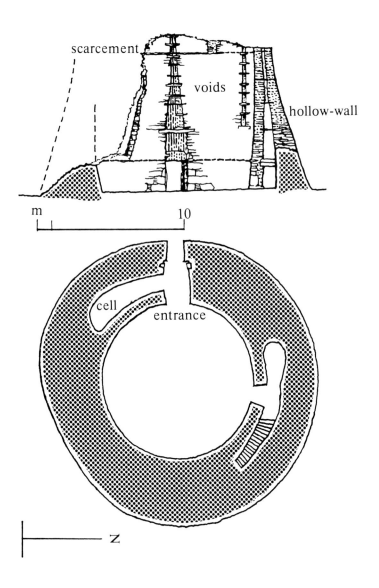

3. Dun Telve, Glenelg, Lochalsh, Highland: plan and cross-section.

2
Brochs and when they were built

The word broch derives from an Old Norse root, *borg,* describing a strong or fortified place; the Gaelic word *dun* is similar, but it is also used to describe hillocks and crags which give the impression of fortified sites, even though they may not be occupied by one.

Several features of broch architecture may be illustrated by detailed examination of Dun Telve, Glenelg, Lochalsh, Highland, a site that shows both on plan and in section many of the components of the idealised broch (figures 2 to 5). Brochs are circular drystone structures enclosing an area measuring between 9 and 12 metres (30 and 40 feet) in diameter, within a wall some 4.5 metres (15 feet) in thickness. The outer walls are always built with a distinct inward batter, giving the profile of the broch its characteristic cooling-tower shape. Because of the care with which the entrance passage was constructed (as the only opening to the interior it was most at risk from attack), this is often one of the best preserved features. The outer part may be about 0.75 metres (2 feet 6 inches) in width and in some cases stands to a height of 1.6 metres (5 feet 3 inches) with the lintel, the horizontal stone over the entrance, often one of the largest to be used in the construction of the broch. In several cases massive blocks with a triangular outer face have been set in position as lintels, and this adds to the impressive nature of the entrance. A short way down the passage the position of a stout wooden door is indicated by the door-checks (or jambs) against which it was closed. In some cases the jambs take the form of upright slabs set into the thickness of the passage wall; in others the drystone walling has been set back a little way from the line of the outer part of the passage. A transverse kerbstone sometimes provides additional support for the door at floor level. The wooden doors do not survive, but in a few examples the pivot stones on which they swung have been discovered. The doors would have been bolted into position by draw-bars of timber, which could be pulled across behind them at night or during attack. The presence of such draw-bars is indicated by a deep slot constructed within the thickness of the wall, in which the beam was housed, and by an opposing socket designed to hold the end of the bar when it was pulled shut.

Behind the door at Dun Telve, on the south side of the passage, there is a guard-cell in the thickness of the wall, measuring some

5.5 metres (18 feet) in length and up to 1.5 metres (5 feet) in width. Another feature of many brochs is the staircase that leads from a chamber or gallery at ground level to the upper parts of the wall and eventually to the top of the broch; one section of the stairway at Dun Telve survives intact.

The hollow-wall construction that is one of the main elements of the classic broch appears to be designed to allow the builders to achieve as great a height as possible without adding dispro-portionately to the weight of the wall, as well perhaps as obviating the necessity for scaffolding during the building. Thus brochs comprise two thicknesses of drystone walling, bonded by cross-slabs at regular intervals, which form galleries within the wall to which access is made possible by the slab-built staircases (figure 4). Such staircases, however, mean that the galleries are not continuous for the stair effectively blocks them; this under-lines the structural function of the double thickness of walling, although some of the rough internal galleries were doubtless used for storage. Only at Mousa, in Shetland, is the staircase continuous from the first gallery to the wall-head.

4. Dun Telve, Glenelg, Lochalsh, Highland, showing hollow wall construction.

5. Dun Telve, Glenelg, Lochalsh, Highland. The entrance passage and void from the interior of the broch.

There are two main types of wall construction, *ground-galleried* and *solid-based*; this distinction is of some importance when considering the main theories of broch evolution. As the name implies, ground-galleried brochs use hollow-wall construction from the basal courses upwards (as at Dun Mor Vaul, Tiree), whereas solid-based brochs (such as Dun Telve) have a thick foundation level (sometimes containing cells or guard-chambers), on which the hollow-walled upper storeys are built. At Dun Telve the wall still stands to a height of about 10 metres (33 feet) with four complete galleries and one fragmentary gallery still visible above the solid base. Dun Telve is one of the tallest surviving brochs. Less usual features, also illustrated at Dun Telve, are two voids or vertical openings in the inner face of the broch wall, one rising above the entrance passage (figure 5), the other on the north-west quadrant. Such voids were in part to lessen the weight of the wall and, as at Dun Telve, for example, were sometimes designed to relieve the weight over the lintel of the inner end of the passage. They may also have been intended to allow air and light into the upper galleries or storage areas.

One other distinctive feature remains to be described — the ledge or scarcement; this is either a setting of stones jutting out from the wall-face or a shelf set back into the wall, which runs horizontally round the interior of the broch. At Dun Telve (and also at Mousa) there are two ledges, one at the same height as the likely position of the door lintels (2 metres; 6 feet 6 inches) and the other at a height of some 9 metres (30 feet). These ledges were almost certainly intended to support the structural timbers of buildings that were set against the broch wall; in a few modern excavations rings of post-holes have also been discovered, and it is likely that the upper scarcement at Dun Telve was designed to support the sort of roof shown in Alan Sorrell's reconstruction drawing of such buildings at Clickhimin, in Shetland (figure 6).

The whole of the interior of some brochs was probably roofed over with turf or thatch, with the supporting joists resting on the upper scarcements and with openings to allow the smoke from the fire to escape. The interior would have been much darker than it appears today and thus more comparable to the interior of the houses of the north and west before the advent of paraffin lamps in the nineteenth century. Many activities such as weaving or pot-making would have been carried on out of doors.

Radiocarbon dates from a small number of brochs indicate that they were built and in use during the first century BC and the first century AD. The chronological table on page 15 shows that this

6. Reconstruction drawing by Alan Sorrell of timber ranges in the interior of Clickhimin broch, Shetland, during the wheel-house period.

was a period of change throughout Britain, and it is possible that some of these events had direct or indirect effects on the far north and west. The influx of the *Belgae* into south-east England in the early first century BC may have instigated tribal movements which have sometimes been thought to have had an effect further north. News of Caesar's expeditions of 55-4 BC may have filtered north, as must surely that of Aulus Plautius in AD 43. Agricola's march into Scotland in AD 81, culminating in the defeat of the *Caledones,* and the circumnavigation of Britain by the Roman fleet in AD 83-4 must have created uncertainty and tension in those areas beyond the boundaries of the Roman Empire. The sight of the fleet in northern and western waters must have aroused considerable unease among the native tribes. (It is worth stressing that accounts of the submission of the *Orcades* to the Emperor Claudius, although frequently quoted, are now thought to reflect an incorrect interpretation of the original sources.) In the course of the circumnavigation of Britain the fleet is said to have 'found and conquered islands, hitherto unknown, which are called the *Orcades'* (Tacitus, *Agricola,* x). The fleet, or part of it, may well have made landfall in Orkney, but there was scarcely time for a campaign; any annexation of the islands is more likely to have been a political assumption than a military reality. There is certainly no reason to link brochs with the Romans, because brochs were being built long before any notion of danger from Roman forces arose in the north. The idea that brochs were built as a protection against Roman slave-taking has an attractive neatness but its chronology is imperfect. This was the conjecture behind Mollie Hunter's novel *The Stronghold,* but, that aside, her story is a powerful evocation of the society in which the concept of the broch emerged — a society in which slave-trading was almost certainly practised, but quite independent of Roman innovation.

This still leaves open the question of why brochs were built. The honest answer is that we do not know. The reasonable assumption is that they were designed to protect and to impress. Intertribal strife between the various sections of the iron age population necessitated local strongholds. Indeed the fact that so few brochs give any impression of having been sacked suggests that this form of fortification was a successful deterrent against attack by warring bands. Prolonged siege would clearly triumph over them, but as protection against short-lived attack, the sort of warfare endemic in iron age society, brochs were ideal.

Nevertheless, the Roman presence does seem to have had a

North & West Scotland	Historical Events
	200 —
BROCHS UNDER CONSTRUCTION	100 — Beginning of Belgic immigrations into south-east England
	Expeditions of Julius Caesar to southern England (55-54BC)
	BC __ AD Claudian invasion under Aulus Plautius (AD43)
	Agricolan campaigns in Scotland 100 (AD79 or 80 – 83 or 84)
	Antonine frontier in southern Scotland (AD142 – c. 163)
many brochs abandoned	200 — Severan campaigns in Scotland (AD208-11)
wheel-houses	300 —
	Barbarian Conspiracy (AD367)
	400 —

marginal effect upon broch building. A glance at the distribution map (figure 1) shows that there is a scattering of brochs far beyond the main area of concentration, with examples in Angus, Fife, the Borders and the south-west of Scotland. The best preserved example is Edinshall, in Berwickshire, one of the largest brochs, with an internal diameter of 17 metres (55 feet 9 inches). Such an apparently anomalous distribution of brochs has allowed archaeologists to speculate on the explanation for the 'intrusion' of brochs into areas of quite different fort-building tradition, and the discovery of Roman objects has allowed the date of such intrusions or invasions to be linked to the various Roman occupations of southern Scotland. At Torwoodlee the broch appears to have been built and demolished during the period between the first and second Roman occupations of Scotland (about AD 100-39); alternatively a date between the later second century AD (after the Romans had gone for the second time) and the Severan advance of AD 209 has been proposed. Both wholesale invasion from the north and gradual infiltration of northern tribesmen have been envisaged. The final publications of excavations at Leckie and Buchlyvie, in Stirling Council, both of which have furnished sequences of radiocarbon dates, will allow this interesting problem to be put into proper context. Leckie is one of the few brochs to have been destroyed as a result of an intensive conflagration.

7. Midhowe, Orkney. Combs used in weaving or in carding wool (scale approximately 1:2).

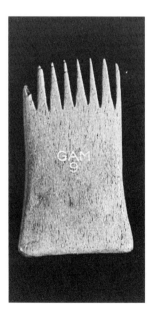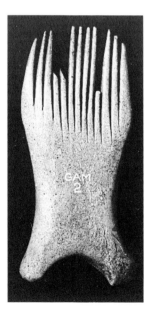

3
Broch economy

In southern and eastern parts of Britain iron age settlements and fortifications are characterised by round-houses (built of timber in the east and of stone and timber in the west) and by hilltop defensive sites, sometimes of great size or structural complexity. In the north and west of Scotland the settlement pattern is different, in large part because arable land is found in small parcels, perhaps at the head of a small bay, perhaps as a coastal strip, with moorland or mountainous tracts between. Communication between the islands and the western mainland was by sea and a good anchorage is often an indicator of prehistoric settlement. In a society fragmented by geographical circumstances large-scale fortifications have a less important role than in other more open regions, although there are a few stone-walled forts, which, because of their greater internal areas, may represent tribal centres of some standing. It is likely, however, that society was structured in a very similar way to that of other parts of Britain. Ptolemy's *Geography*, compiled between AD 140 and 150, gives the names of some of the Celtic tribal units, although it is not precise about which parts of Scotland they occupied. It was probably a tribal society, something akin to that outlined in Irish tales with kings, bards and warriors, the economy depending on mixed farming, with hunting and fishing playing important roles.

Stone-walled fortifications were being constructed by the middle of the first millennium BC and there followed a long period of structural experimentation with stone and with timber-lacing to increase the stability of the wall. When a timber-laced fort caught fire, either by accident or in the course of attack, the beams caught light and in certain conditions appear to have acted as flues allowing great heat to be generated, with the resultant fusing (or vitrifaction) of the wall core. Timber-laced fortifications were certainly being constructed before the time that brochs were being put up (though the technique was also used at later dates). In the later part of the iron age, however, smaller defensive structures were far more common — these are represented by duns in the west and by brochs in the north-west and north. Duns are small drystone forts, which share some of the structural features of brochs — checked entrances, guard-cells and mural features — but do not have the all-round hollow-wall

8. Whalebone vessel from Cinn Trolla, Sutherland, Highland (scale about 1:4).

9. An Orcadian girl grinds corn with a rotary quern in the late nineteenth century.

construction or the height of the latter. In a few cases duns overlie earlier forts, and this, together with finds from a few excavated examples, suggests that they are in essence stoutly defended homesteads of about the first century AD, though it is clear that some were also in use at rather later dates. It is likely that not all brochs were as tall as Dun Telve, and thus many of the duns of Argyll may originally have been as impressive architecturally as many of the northern brochs to which they are closely related. Other types of structure include the *aisled round-house* and *wheel-house*: both are small circular stone-built houses with radiating piers of masonry to help to support the roof. In the former the piers are free-standing, set about half-way between the inner wall and the centre of the house (where there was often a hearth); in the latter the piers project from the inner face of the wall in the manner of the spokes of a cart-wheel.

The evidence about the economy of the broch of Midhowe, on Rousay, one of the major islands of Orkney, is fuller than from many other excavated brochs and it provides information about many aspects of broch life. The bones of domesticated animals include cattle, sheep and pig; hunting is represented by red and roe deer, wild cat and fox. Fowling also played a part, for goose, duck and heron bones were recovered. It is likely that fishing also made a contribution to the economy. The wool from sheep was spun and woven, for spindle whorls and bone or antler combs (figure 7), used either in weaving or in carding wool preparatory to weaving, were found. Many points, pins and spatulae show the importance of bone implements; whalebone was also used in the manufacture of cups (figure 8) and tools. Deerhorn was used to make hammer-heads, hafts and handles. Stonework included whetstones and hollowed cups or lamps as well as both saddle and rotary querns (figure 9). There were large quantities of hammer-stones and pounders. Bronze-working is represented by ring-headed pins (figure 10) and brooches; there was also a large quantity of iron slag, though iron tools have not themselves survived. Pottery vessels include large, comparatively plain storage jars and cooking vessels (figure 11). Objects that indicate trading or exchange include fragments of Roman pottery and pieces of a Roman bronze *patera*. Games of chance are indicated by the discovery of dice or counters at many brochs.

There is little evidence for warlike activity on any site – few weapons have been discovered and there is no evidence for the burning or slighting of any broch, except Leckie, Stirling, and Torwoodlee, Scottish Borders, where the wall may have

10. (Left) Bone and bronze pins from Midhowe, Orkney (scale approximately 1:2).
11. (Right) Pottery vessel from Midhowe, Orkney (scale approximately 1:4).

been deliberately dismantled. The picture is of comparatively well-to-do farmers based in stoutly defended brochs, presumably in contact both with neighbouring groups within a wider tribal framework, as well as with the native and Roman worlds to the south. Only the few brochs in the southern parts of Scotland occur in areas that were at any time subjected to Roman rule. Perhaps, like the fortified manor houses at the centre of many medieval English settlements, which were surely rarely attacked, brochs were symbols of prestige and preparedness.

Excavations at two sites in Shetland illustrate the building of a broch within a structural sequence, and, although the brochs of the far north are not perhaps the earliest, Jarlshof and Clickhimin have produced important evidence about the relationship of brochs to earlier and later structures which complements the economic evidence outlined in this chapter.

4
Jarlshof, Clickhimin and Mousa

The brochs of Shetland are among the most visually arresting
prehistoric monuments in Scotland — Mousa enjoying a position,
not altogether justified, as the archetypal broch. Three sites are
of particular interest: the reports on excavations at Jarlshof and
Clickhimin by J. R. C. Hamilton have had a profound effect on
the way that the northern iron age has been presented, while the
superb preservation of Mousa places it in a unique position.

Jarlshof is situated near the southern tip of Shetland, a location
that furnishes a fine natural harbour, fertile soils for agriculture
and pasture, fresh water springs and a ready supply of good
stone. Although only one half of the broch survives, the other
having been destroyed by the sea, the site is important because of
the sequence of structures that successive campaigns of excavation have revealed. Earlier than the broch are stone-built houses
of later neolithic, bronze age and early iron age date; some are of
cellular construction, with small cubicles opening from a central
paved area which contains a hearth. Circular in plan (figure 12),
the broch has an internal diameter of 9 metres (29 feet 6 inches)
within a solid-based wall about 5.2 metres (17 feet) thick, which
rises with an external batter to a height of about 3 metres (10
feet). There are two opposed cells, both of which have been
partly breached by the sea (there is no evidence that the west cell
was part of the entrance arrangements as has sometimes been
suggested). The entrance was presumably in the seaward half.
The inner face of the broch is vertical with a well preserved
scarcement at a height of some 2.3 metres (7 feet 6 inches).
Within the interior there is a well at least 4 metres (13 feet) in
depth, which was sunk into the underlying bedrock. The broch
was cleared out at the beginning of the twentieth century and
nothing was found that might help reconstruct the internal
arrangements. A small number of artefacts was recovered,
including cooking vessels with everted rims and a bone weaving-
comb. The broch was not, however, a totally isolated structure
for it is associated with a large courtyard protected by a wall still
over 3 metres (10 feet) in height. There is a cell within the
thickness of the broch wall, but the main entrance must have
been in that portion destroyed by the sea.

The sequence of domestic structures later than the broch is
perhaps the most exciting part of prehistoric Jarlshof: set in the

north-west part of the courtyard, the earliest is an aisled round-house, originally about 9.7 metres (32 feet) in internal diameter; a series of free-standing piers, perhaps replacing an earlier arrangement of timber uprights, divided it into a number of compartments around a central open area containing the hearth. Later several wheel-houses were constructed, one within the broch itself, one overlying part of the aisled round-house and another occupying a large part of the remaining courtyard. The corbelled stone piers radiating from the inner wall-face, which still stands to a height of about 3 metres (10 feet), demonstrate that the architectural skills of the descendants of the broch-builders were in no way diminished.

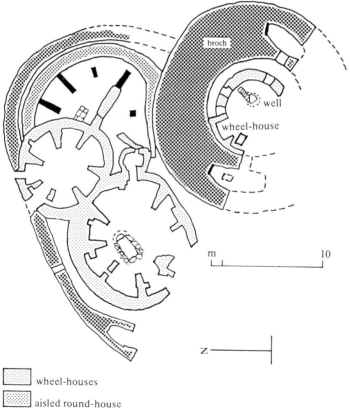

12. Jarlshof, Shetland: plan of broch and wheel-houses.

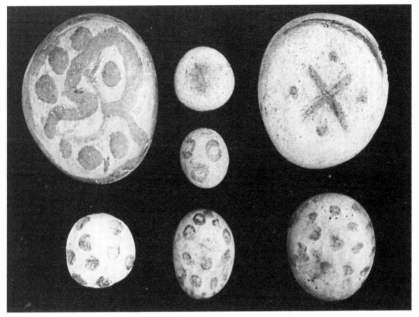

13. Painted pebbles from a number of different brochs; perhaps they are charm stones, or have a religious significance, or were used in games.

A greater range of artefacts was recovered from the aisled round-house than from the broch; these included tools of slate, pins and awls of bone, saddle querns, stone pounders and fragments of decorated pottery vessels with steatite grit. The finds indicate an economy based on fishing and seal-hunting combined with mixed farming. The excavator suggested that the pottery belonged to 'a lower order of society brought down the peninsula as a labour force for the construction of the broch tower; a body of people who, on the completion of their work, decided to settle in the high-walled courtyard'. But such an interpretation is at best speculative. There are several innovations in the material found in the wheel-house levels, including rotary querns, a quartz pebble painted with eyebrow and spot decoration (comparable to those in figure 13), small bone spoons and a new and distinctive style of pottery — red, hard-fired vessels (with no steatite grits) with flat, roll-top or bead rims. Such cooking pots can be paralleled widely in broch and post-broch contexts in Orkney. Only one segment of the history of Jarlshof is summarised here, the later prehistoric, Viking and Late Norse phases falling beyond the span of this volume.

The fort and broch of Clickhimin are situated on what is now a small promontory jutting into the Loch of Clickhimin in the western suburbs of Lerwick (figure 14). The remains are well preserved and excavations have allowed a detailed sequence of construction to be proposed. The excavations have also revealed a large number of objects as well as evidence about the economy of the people who lived there. When occupation of the site began, the Loch of Clickhimin would have been open to the sea, but the creation of a storm-beach across the mouth of the sea-loch led to the damming of the loch during the later first millennium BC, and this brought about a rise in the water level of the loch itself, with disastrous results.

Seven main periods of building have been proposed. The earliest is a small farmstead of late bronze age date (about 700 BC) comprising a thick-walled house with a cell let into the wall and a central hearth. The islet may later have been the site of a small farmstead, which was completely destroyed by the building of the broch, but the evidence for this period is largely conjectural. In the third period a large drystone wall was drawn round the margin of the islet enclosing an area about 42 by 38 metres (138 by 125 feet), measuring up to 3.6 metres (12 feet) in thickness and still standing to a height of 1.7 metres (5 feet 6 inches). The wall was probably thickest on the south-east side where there was an entrance. The inner face of the wall was used to support ranges of timber buildings, some of which were used as cattle byres.

One of the most remarkable structures of the pre-broch periods at Clickhimin, but one whose chronological position within the sequence is open to several interpretations, is the block-house: a free-standing drystone gateway set just within the entrance to the fort. Hamilton suggests that the original intention of the builders was that the block-house was to be the main entrance to the fort, and that the walls would have linked up to the sides of this impressive feature, but that for some reason the decision was taken to enclose a larger area and the detached block-house was not incorporated. Dr E. W. MacKie, however, has proposed that the block-house is the gateway of a second pre-broch fort, perhaps never completed. The block-house itself is of puzzling construction, a segment of a fortification, as though only part of the plan had been completed, like knitting only the front of a pullover. It is some 13 metres (42 feet 6 inches) in overall length

14. Aerial view of Clickhimin, Shetland.

and is bowed on ground-plan with a central entrance passage. There was a doorway at a point about 1.5 metres (5 feet) from the outside which was secured by a draw-bar; the deep socket in which it was housed is still visible on the west side. Within the thickness of the walls on either side of the entrance passage there are small cells that can be entered only from above and perhaps served as pit-prisons. On the inner wall of the block-house, at a height of about 2.4 metres (8 feet) above ground level, there are the remains of a projecting scarcement course; on the analogy of brochs, it is likely that the block-house supported a timber structure, though there is little other evidence for this apart from an internal area of cobbling. The reconstruction of the timber work as a two-storeyed building is at best optimistic.

The pre-broch phase of fortification was of extended duration, and reconstruction is certainly to be expected; during this time the inland loch was naturally formed and the resultant rise in water level also led to changes in building. The finds show a mixed economy of arable and pastoral farming as well as fishing.

The large tower of a solid-based broch, measuring some 9 metres (30 feet) in diameter within a wall up to 6.5 metres (21 feet

4 inches) thick, is the dominant feature of the site, with the main entrance on the west flank; the void above the inner end of the passage may be compared with that at Dun Telve. There are two cells within the thickness of the wall, one on the north-east and the other, not now accessible, on the south. There was a scarcement some 2 metres (6 feet 6 inches) above the floor level, and excavation revealed the sockets for upright posts by which internal timber buildings were supported. Unusually there are two other subsidiary entrances into the broch, both at upper levels. The one on the north leads not only into the interior but also to the staircase to the wall-head; it is surely no accident that there is an unusual heel of stonework on the outer wall face just beneath it. The second entrance leads to an intra-mural gallery. Finds from the broch include stone lamps, whetstones, bone and whalebone objects, a die and a few bronze objects; the pottery finds are characterised by cooking pots with decorated neck bands.

Finally, the interior of the broch was used as a wheel-house. Although the radiating stone piers no longer survive, they were carefully described in the nineteenth century; the wall of the wheel-house itself can still be seen as well as the single cell within it. The excavations of 1861-2 showed that there was a hearth at its centre.

Several aspects of broch architecture are echoed by the block-house at Clickhimin (scarcement ledge and door arrangements), but these may also be paralleled on several duns and it is not necessary to see this particular structure as being ancestral to the broch. Rather, it and the other block-house forts of Shetland, including Loch of Huxter, Ness of Burgi and Scatness, illustrate a desire for gateways designed to impress and are perhaps best seen as an indication of local experimentation in fort-building techniques.

On 9th August 1814 Sir Walter Scott went ashore on the island of Mousa to 'see the very ancient castle of Mousa, which stands close to the sea-shore. It is a Pictish fortress, the most entire probably in the world. In form it resembles a dice-box, for the truncated cone is continued only to a certain height, after which it begins to rise perpendicularly ...'. There is no doubt that Mousa is one of the major architectural achievements of prehistoric Britain (figures 15 and 16). The solid-based wall, some 5.5 metres (18 feet) thick, encloses an area about 5.5 metres (18 feet) in internal diameter. It is the startling height to which the broch survives that places it in a class apart, for it is some 13.3 metres

15. Mousa, Shetland.

(43 feet 6 inches). The entrance passage was partly reconstructed in the nineteenth century, but the position of the doorway and the bar-hole can still be seen. There are three large cells within the basal course of the wall. These are entered across thresholds which are internally 0.7 metres (2 feet 4 inches) above the floor levels; above the entrance the walls are pierced by openings to let air and presumably light into the cells, although as the openings are below scarcement level they were probably covered by internal timber buildings. The cells all have little aumbries or cupboards set into the thickness of the wall.

Above the solid base there are five galleries below the present wall-head walk, which is reached by a continuous staircase. The galleries, to which ready access is effectively blocked by the staircase, are partly lit by three voids. The twin scarcement ledges, at heights of 2.1 and 3.7 metres (6 feet 10 inches and 12 feet 2 inches) above floor level, show there were originally ranges of timber buildings within the broch. Like so many other brochs, the interior of Mousa is masked by secondary structures, including an inner skin of walling, a hearth and a stone-lined tank.

The excellent state of preservation of Mousa must reflect the high standard of building, its comparative isolation and the absence of large-scale building nearby which saved it from being used as a quarry; the adjacent shore provided an easier and safer supply of stones for the later farm and field-walls. But the major factor in its preservation is surely that the internal diameter of the broch is unusually small, although the wall thickness is quite normal, providing the structure with unusual cohesion.

It has been estimated that out of a possible hundred brochs in Shetland 75 survive. In drawing attention to only three broch sites

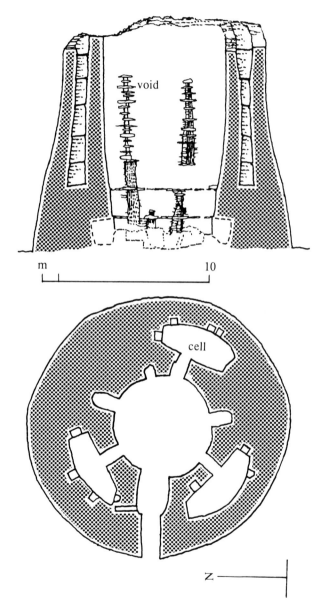

16. Mousa, Shetland: plan and section.

in Shetland there is a danger of underestimating other forms of iron age settlement and fortification, but by underlining the importance of the sequences of building at Clickhimin and Jarlshof an attempt has been made to illustrate earlier and later building types (stone-walled forts, aisled round-houses and wheel-houses). Other classes, including small duns, are also present in Shetland.

Coastal erosion prompted the most recent campaign of excavations, including a structure at Scatness 400 metres (437 yards) north of Ness of Burgi, limited excavation at Ness of Burgi, and the brochs at East Shore and Burland. Housing developments at Upper Scalloway revealed unexpectedly the presence of a broch, and this has been excavated in advance of development. At Scatness only the eastern half of the 'block-house' survived, most of the western half having been lost in the process of erosion, but it was clearly very comparable in construction to that of Ness of Burgi. Only a few sherds of pottery were found, and unfortunately the radiocarbon dates refer to periods after its abandonment. In the course of this work the pottery from Ness of Burgi was re-examined in the light of work being undertaken at Kebister, north of Lerwick, and a date between 200 BC and AD 200 was proposed.

Current interpretations stress the unsuitable position of structures such as Ness of Burgi and Scatness as defensive fortifications and prefer to see their construction as creating symbolic backdrops to ritualised warfare or as gateways to be passed through in *rites de passage*. The practicalities of many rock- or cliff-girt stone-walled structures are difficult to understand, and statements of prestige and authority may have been as important for many as the defensible possibilities of any site.

Chronological evidence from the East Shore broch was limited, but it was suggested that it was almost certainly built before or during the early centuries AD.

17. Aerial view of Gurness, Orkney.
18. Bu, Orkney: central area in the course of excavation.

5
Orkney and Caithness

The most recent developments in broch studies have taken place
in Orkney, with the excavations at Bu and Howe, both near
Stromness, on the western side of Mainland. This is appropriate,
for it is in Orkney and Caithness that we come closest to
understanding the landscape of the broch period and to achieving
an overall picture of settlement archaeology. This is because
brochs in this area are frequently surrounded by contemporary
domestic settlements, so that the brochs are not isolated from the
communities that supported them. Huge grass-grown mounds
still cover the remains of many brochs, even some of those that
were badly excavated in the nineteenth century, but two in
Orkney stand clear of debris: Midhowe on Rousay and Gurness
on Mainland, both belonging to a series of brochs lining the
shores of Eynhallow Sound. The interiors of both brochs are
furnished in stone with partitions, hearths, tanks and other
fittings that would elsewhere have been made of wood, and both
have stone-built domestic structures outside the towers. Midhowe
has already been described in chapter 3; like Gurness, it is a
ground-galleried broch with strong outer defences.

Gurness in its heyday must have been a remarkable sight. The
remains are so well preserved that it is not difficult to picture the
smooth broch tower rising above an apron of semi-detached
houses, the whole encircled by ramparts and ditches to create a
fortified village (figure 17). The growth of Gurness is not entirely
understood, but the basic sequence is clear enough and is likely to
be typical of other complex broch sites: the broch and its outlying
defences were built first, then domestic houses were fitted into
the space between broch and rampart, leaving a passageway
round the broch and from the broch entrance out to the causeway
through the defences. Successive modifications, both to the
houses and to the broch interior, show that this village phase
lasted many years; datable finds suggest perhaps three hundred
years, from the first or second century AD to the third or fourth
century. Dating is, for brochs, typically imprecise. During this
time, the broch itself became redundant as a defensive structure,
and eventually the whole settlement fell into decay. New
buildings, probably using the old broch tower as a handy source
of stone, rose on top of the levelled ruins, probably in the seventh
century AD. These may properly be called Pictish (chapter 8) and

belong to post-broch history, as do the traces of ninth-century Viking activity on the site, but they demonstrate the way in which an old broch sometimes remained a focus for settlement in later centuries.

Excavations at Bu and Howe have helped to clarify both the basic sequence demonstrated at Gurness and the local developments behind the origin of brochs. At Bu, rescue excavation revealed a structure some 9.1 metres (29 feet 10 inches) in internal diameter within a wall originally some 3.6 metres (11 feet 9 inches) thick, to which an outer skin was later added, thus increasing the thickness to 5.2 metres (17 feet). The entrance passage contained a door-check, but there were no guard-cells. The internal arrangements at Bu were startlingly complete – with a large hearth and a cooking tank at the centre. The outer portion of the interior was divided by radiating walls or upright slabs into a series of cubicles, and these walls also had a part to play in supporting the roof (figure 18). The radiocarbon dates from the site show that the occupation was taking place around 600 BC, much earlier than might have been expected for a structure that must surely be ancestral to brochs; even earlier dates from a round-house at Quanterness, however, underline the long sequence of structural experimentation in Orkney.

This impression of a gradual development from round-house to broch is further emphasised by the evidence from Howe, where there were two phases in the building of the broch itself. The first is a solid-based structure, with an unusual and not at all broch-like entrance passage with cells on either side of it and two opposing staircases within the wall; the internal arrangements suggest that the interior was subdivided by seven radial partitions, and a ring of post-holes shows that there were inner timber ranges. After the collapse of this structure, a second was built, a massive solid-based tower with a long entrance passage and a single cell and staircase; the interior was subdivided by radial partitions. The broch itself appears to have been used for storage purposes, but a settlement of stone-built houses, each one provided with a hearth and a 'tank' made of four slabs, are thought to be contemporary. The excavation report well illustrates the complexities of disentangling the structural sequence from the mass of tumbled rubble created by continued building and rebuilding on the same spot.

John Hedges has listed some 52 certain brochs and as many as eighty possible examples in Orkney, and he has analysed the diagnostic features; most are solid-based with only a few ground-galleried examples (or at least ground-galleried in part). Where information exists the entrances may be seen to conform with brochs elsewhere, with the provision of door-checks and guard-cells. At least ten of the Orkney brochs are provided with wells. Unfortunately many of the brochs of Orkney and Caithness were dug into in Victorian times with little regard for the recording of where objects were found. Sir Francis Tress-Barry dug as many as fifteen between 1891 and 1904 along the coast of Caithness, a speed hardly suited to careful recording. Before the advent of radiocarbon dating, the Orkney sites were particularly important in dating brochs generally, for several yielded datable Roman imports that demonstrated occupation in the early centuries AD. Their internal furnishings of stone are a rich source of information about how brochs were used; although some may represent secondary modifications, Hedges has convincingly shown that, in several cases, these carefully designed interiors are original to the construction of the brochs.

The dense distribution of brochs in Caithness and Sutherland (there may be as many as two hundred in Caithness alone) can be seen from the distribution map (figure 1), but only two, Crosskirk and Carn Liath, have been dug in recent times. The former was excavated in advance of destruction by coastal erosion and no longer survives, but the complexities of this interesting excavation, including a wide range of radiocarbon dates, underline the importance of this area to broch studies. Carn Liath, however, is well worth visiting because the entrance passage is still lintelled and the door-checks, bar-hole and guard-cell remain intact. Like so many brochs, it was the focus of secondary occupation both in the interior and outside. Although many Caithness brochs have been dug to some extent in the past, most have been filled in again and there is little structural detail to be seen. An exception is the complex known as the Wag of Forse, where there are the upstanding remains of a broch (with a fine quadrangular lintel over the main entrance) and of the oblong houses belonging to the Early Historic period that replaced it.

19. General view of Dun Ardtreck, Skye.

20. General view of Dun Carloway, Lewis, Western Isles.

6
Skye and the Western Isles

The brochs of Skye and adjacent areas of the mainland have an important role as they form part of one of the most convincing patterns of evolution of this distinctive building tradition. Outlined by Dr E. W. MacKie, the theory of development stresses the presence of D-shaped fortifications built against the edge of a cliff or precipice, which have been constructed using a hollow-wall technique. Such fortifications, or semibrochs, as Dun Grugaig in Glenelg, Dun Ardtreck in Skye and Dun an Ruigh Ruaidh on Loch Broom in Wester Ross, may be seen as prototype brochs, the sort of structure from which the true circular broch developed. Excavations undertaken at two semi-brochs have produced radiocarbon dates which show that they were built in the first or second centuries BC — certainly as early as most brochs and probably earlier. Dun Ardtreck is a strongly built D-shaped fort, with sheer cliffs falling some 21 metres (70 feet) to the sea forming the chord of the D; the safety of the inhabitants seems to dictate that there was originally a protective screen to stop people falling off the seaward side. The entrance was particularly well preserved with door-checks characteristic of brochs (figure 19). Dun Ardtreck was constructed with a rudimentary hollow-wall. If such semibrochs are indeed to be seen as the precursors of true broch-building traditions, it is perhaps not surprising that the brochs of the Western Isles, Skye and the adjacent mainland demonstrate such assured building technique. Dun Carloway on Lewis (figure 20), Dun Beag on Skye, Dun Troddan and Dun Telve in Glenelg stand out amongst the finest brochs of the west. Sadly, however, their excavation did not produce an extensive range of small finds that might be compared to that outlined from Midhowe, but it is likely that the social and economic basis was very similar.

The excavation of Dun Mor Vaul, Tiree, by Dr E. W. MacKie between 1962 and 1964 marks the beginning of modern research into the brochs of Atlantic Scotland. It is a fascinating site to visit as so many of the features of the 'classic' broch can clearly be seen and, as a result of the excavation, a detailed sequence of construction and occupation can be demonstrated (figures 21 and 22). The broch measures 9.2 metres (30 feet 2 inches) in internal diameter within a well built wall some 4.5 metres (14 feet 9 inches) in thickness; the inner face is as much as 1.4 metres (4 feet

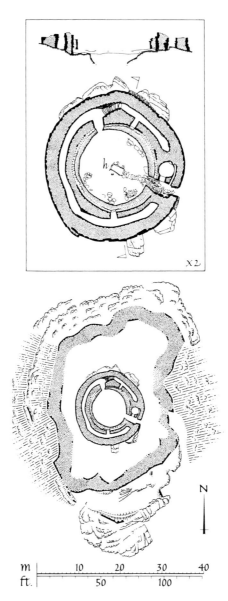

21. Dun Mor Vaul, Tiree, Argyll and Bute, plan and section.

22. Dun Mor Vaul, Tiree, Argyll and Bute, interior of broch.

7 inches) in height with a distinct ledge or scarcement at a height of 1.4 metres (4 feet 7 inches). The entrance on the south-east flank has checks to secure the door as well as a bar-hole. Just inside the door there is a corbelled guard-cell leading from the north side of the passage. The intra-mural gallery is still well preserved and the staircase, which allowed access to the upper levels, is situated on the north. The site was additionally protected by a rough wall drawn round the margin of the rocky knoll on which the broch is situated. Two periods of occupation of the site pre-date the construction of the broch in the first century AD; subsequently the broch was partly dismantled and was used for domestic occupation, its function as a defensive stronghold abandoned. The roof of this house may have been supported at least in part on the skin of walling that was added to the inner face. It is likely that the site was abandoned about the middle of the third century AD. The finds from the site included large quantities of pottery, rotary querns, tools and dice of bone, as well as bronze objects. It is clear that both the weaving of wool and working of metals were undertaken on the site.

7
Broch origins

The political and social background of brochs has a particular fascination for Scottish antiquaries, each age evoking its own parallels. In 1935, for example, Gordon Childe wrote: 'Such a concentration and juxtaposition of immensely strong fortresses must reflect peculiar social conditions. Anderson and Curle regard the brochs as a system of defence against sea-raiders. W. Mackenzie and I prefer to explain them as the castles of a conquering aristocracy designed, like the Norman keeps, to overawe a subject population. The effect of blood-feuds such as arise in a clan society, as in Albania today, must also be borne in mind. In any case the broch is eloquent of dangerously unstable conditions under which the farmer and fisherman might at any moment have to retreat into an impregnable refuge. The broch castle, created in the north, was carried south presumably by bands of raiders who settled in those richer lands.'

J. R. C. Hamilton, following his work at Jarlshof and Clickhimin, outlined a sequence for the evolution of fortifications that culminated in the broch, taking the wall types of a number of iron age fort-building traditions as points of origin: timber-laced forts; walls that employ an inner skin of stonework to increase their stability (the *murus duplex* technique); and thirdly fortifications with drystone walls such as the small duns of the Atlantic coast of Scotland. In essence, the addition of internal timber ranges to an outer drystone wall, coupled with a desire to heighten the wall in order to support additional storeys, culminates in a tall hollow-walled tower with internal timber ranges — the broch. While it is indeed possible that internal timber fittings helped to dictate the shape and structure of the encircling drystone wall, it seems particularly unlikely that, as Hamilton argues, this took place in Orkney, where several millennia of building tradition demonstrate the skills of Orcadian architects in a comparatively treeless landscape. MacKie has expressed caution about the interpretation of the post-holes of the pre-broch fort at Clickhimin and about a too ready assumption that the attractive reconstruction drawings of the excavation report are an accurate reflection of the evidence.

One of the most important contributions to broch studies was undertaken by MacKie in 1965, in the course of which he produced a matrix analysis based on four of the vital statistics of

some 120 brochs. The statistics included the proportion of the
diameter measurement that was occupied by the wall-base, the
overall diameter, the geographical area and, if known, the
structural type of the broch (for example, ground-galleried or
solid-based). He has commented that the 'relative massiveness of
the broch's wall-base reflects the original height of the tower and
that the smallest and most massive, Mousa, was the highest',
although in some cases local considerations of geology and
topography may have a part to play.

Both Sir Lindsay Scott and J. R. C. Hamilton make use of the
relationship between timber and stone as building materials in
their different evolutionary sequences. This is a will o' the wisp
subject, for the evidence is at best fugitive or negative, and in
only a few excavations is there much useful information from
post-holes. In both approaches the builders 'make do' with stone
when what they would have preferred were ready supplies of
timber — the steady transformation of an ideal until a satisfactory
stone-built structure is achieved. Such evolutionary theories, in
both cases involving incoming folk to act as catalysts, do little
justice to the long-standing skills in stone of the indigenous
inhabitants. Post-holes associated with the occupation of brochs
show that in some cases timber was employed in the construction
of internal buildings, and the notion of timber ranges against the
wall is an attractive one. It is odd that there are no signs of the
sockets by which wooden beams might be bonded more securely
into the wall (in the manner of putlog holes that form a visual
reminder of the wooden cross-members of a medieval tower-
house, for example), for wood and stone were carefully bonded
in timber-laced forts and probably at the gate-towers of many
fortifications.

Many writers on brochs have postulated that an intrusive
element into the population of the west and north was responsible
for the building of such distinctive fortifications (and allied
domestic structures such as aisled round-houses and wheel-
houses). Thus in 1947 Scott made the case that all three types of
structure could be derived from the timber round-houses of
southern Britain, but that in a landscape where good timber was
at a premium constructional features were transformed into
stone. Scott thought that a wave of refugees from the south,
related to the folk whose material culture was known from the
Glastonbury lake-villages, made their way up the west coast into
the Hebrides. He was thus able to explain both traits in the
building traditions and similarities in the artefactual evidence

between the two areas. Scott was also of the opinion that the majority of brochs had comparatively low walls, in line with his view that they were really defended houses, and that the tall tower-brochs were not the 'norm'. In 1971 Mackie, in his detailed study of the origins of brochs, concluded: 'We have reasonably good evidence that a number of families, rather than traders, bearing the late Iron Age B (or late Woodbury) culture of the Wessex area settled in the Hebrides just before the earliest ground-galleried brochs appeared, probably on Skye . . . A date of between 80 and 70 BC thus seems a suitable one at present for the first appearance of Wessex refugees in southern Scotland and the Hebrides.'

The notion of folk movements is an attractive one to write about — it makes a readily understood framework for processes of change in structural techniques or in the artefact assemblage, but it is perhaps too easy an answer. Hamilton, in describing the building of the fort at Clickhimin, conjures up the arrival of one such group. 'The penetration into the northern isles of Iron Age crofters, whalers and prospectors content to wrest a living from the machair lands and the sea gave way to more intensive colonisation by larger groups, better organised and equipped to develop a mixed economy and to exploit the advantages of maritime power in the fifth to first centuries BC. This phase witnessed the landing of many groups along the coast, not in isolated family units as in the previous period, but in large, well organised bands, capable of securing beach-heads and of erecting fortifications.' Following his discussion of the archaeological evidence for the origin of hollow-wall architecture in Atlantic Scotland, MacKie speculates (and he states clearly that it is no more than that) about 'the immigrant southerners who saw the possibilities of further development in the indigenous semibrochs already in use on Skye. Remembering perhaps their abandoned round wooden farmhouses with internal raised lofts, they would have realised that if the tall hollow rampart was built as a compact circle an immensely strong, practically impregnable tower would result.'

It is important in archaeology to allow one's imagination to roam and to build theories with the evidence at one's disposal, but also to realise that they are imaginative constructs and have the limitations both of one's own attitudes and of the more general archaeological framework of the day. Theoretical approaches now might try to probe the social or economic background of iron age society rather than to paint patterns of movements or influences with broad-brush strokes or arrows from Wessex, Glastonbury or the continent. In general, archaeologists today are less ready to invoke migrations and refugee movements as explanations for cultural changes; this fashion may in part be a reaction to earlier thinking with the realisation that the uncertainty of much of the evidence makes chronological charts and idealised flow-diagrams of cultural contacts very much a matter of personal preferences. But this is not to deny that folk movements in the iron age did take place, and are indeed historically attested as Caesar's mentions of the *Belgae* and the *Helvetii* show. Nor can archaeological evidence be used to disprove a theory — to say that things did not happen in the way suggested — for frequently aspects of several different approaches may strike chords of agreement. It is thus unhelpful to try to compare Childe's views of 1935, Scott's of 1947 and 1948, or Hamilton's and MacKie's of the 1960s and 1970s, for not only has more information come to light, but also attitudes and ways of presenting the material have altered. Thus, although brochs have been much excavated and studied, the object of speculation and theorising, no one solution as to 'origin' or 'evolution' can be wholly endorsed, though in general the date at which the majority of brochs were being used is now accepted. R. Martlew has summed up his examination of the data with a plea for more information in order to present a sound and relevant classification. Recently J. C. Barrett has taken earlier examinations of broch 'origins' to task. 'Building skills and traditions do develop within a community, and somewhere within Scotland, but only in the terms of our definition, there lies the earliest broch. But if we ever find it, and we will never know if we have, will we really be closer to understanding these monuments?'

The writer used to share MacKie's view of an origin for the hollow-walled broch in the Atlantic west, probably Skye, in about the first century BC, though as a local invention and not one generated by incomers. Indeed MacKie has summed up this approach: 'Those who prefer to see the brochs as the final result of an ancient Scottish fort-building tradition will have no quarrel with the concept that they emerged from the locally developed semibrochs, themselves presumably the end products of several centuries of Hebridean building skill.' But the recent radiocarbon dates from Bu have forced a revision of this view and an early tradition of the building of broch-like structures in Orkney and probably Caithness now seems likely. If incomers (either as warrior chieftains or refugees) are not invoked, and there is little reason to do so, brochs may be seen as the upmarket equivalent of the defended round-house or a range of fortifications including duns, and there is good reason to think that itinerant broch-builders provided an architectural service for local magnates. Thus we should perhaps imagine a fusion of ideas from both the north and west with circular structures such as Bu offering one aspect of the internal layout of brochs and wheel-houses (the compartmentalising of the enclosed floor area), while the early brochs and semibrochs of the Atlantic coast pioneer the hollow-wall construction which made such an important contribution to 'classic' tower brochs such as Mousa and Dun Telve.

Ian Armit has suggested that the term 'Atlantic round-house' be used as an overall term to describe 'the rather confusing typological morass' that includes brochs, duns, galleried duns and semibrochs. This has the advantage of uniting the body of stone-built structures of the north and west of Scotland and of stressing the domestic nature of many of them. Broch towers still remain as a category within the wider framework for the majority of the sites that have been the subject of this volume. The typological complexities remain, however, as the earlier broch-like structure at Howe, Orkney, would be designated a complex round-house, with only the second and more substantial phase warranting the term 'broch tower'. Armit's approach has been important in stressing the elements of domestic prestige involved in broch construction, but those aspects that demonstrate defence should not be overlooked. The problems inherent in trying to straight-jacket unexcavated sites into strict classifications is elegantly resolved.

8
What brochs are not

Several recurrent themes in letters from visitors to Scotland, or those who have discovered brochs for the first time, as well as a series of chronological 'red-herrings' in tourist guides and topographical literature, suggest that three final topics should be pursued. Brochs are not 'Pictish towers' (any more than souterrains are 'Picts' houses'); the building of brochs has no connection with the Vikings; there is nothing to suggest that broch architecture owes anything to the *nuraghi* of Sardinia.

The Picts formed one of the most important of the tribal groupings of that part of Scotland north of the Forth-Clyde isthmus in Early Historic times. From about AD 500, however, that part of the west coast of Scotland that is now Argyll had become part of the kingdom of the Scots, whose homeland lay in Dal Riata, the coastal part of what is now County Antrim in Northern Ireland, but until the advent of the Vikings, first as raiders (from about AD 800) and then as settlers, the whole of the northern part of Scotland may be thought of as Pictish. The Picts themselves are first mentioned in a panegyric by the Roman author Eumenius in AD 297, but it is unlikely that they used this term themselves at this time. What is clear is that the various separate iron age tribes had consolidated into a larger grouping, doubtless in part as a result of Roman presence in the south. Thus to use the term 'Pictish' for structures that were built rather earlier than the first use of the term is a misleading anachronism — the more so because it can create an impression that brochs are contemporary with the magnificent sculptured stones that we rightly think of as Pictish. Some ruined broch sites were, however, occupied by the Picts and the rubble was used to build secondary settlements that we can describe as 'Pictish'; examples of such later settlements include Burrian, Gurness and Howe in Orkney. It is better to give credit to the Picts for the achievement of their sculpture and to their unnamed predecessors for the creation of the broch.

For similar reasons we must not think of brochs as 'Viking' or 'Norse'. Viking settlement began to take place from around AD 800, by which time brochs had long gone out of use, but the Vikings recognised them as forts and gave them the name we know today. The broch of Mousa is one of the few prehistoric sites whose name is recorded in the Norse sagas, for Egil's Saga tells of a couple eloping from Norway to Iceland in about AD 900, who were shipwrecked in Shetland and made the broch 'Moseyjarborg' a temporary refuge. The Orkneyinga Saga contains the story of the abduction by Erlend of Margaret, mother of Earl Harald Maddadson, in 1153; Erlend, Margaret and his followers took up a defensive position in the broch, which he had already provisioned, and although Earl Harald followed the fugitives and laid siege to the broch, the saga tells that he found it 'an unhandy place to get at'. (There was, however, a happy ending and the marriage between Erlend and Margaret was allowed to take place.)

The brochs of the Western Isles did not lose their positions as strongholds, for one traditional tale records the use of the broch of Carloway in the seventeenth century during a dispute between the Morrisons of Ness and the Macaulays of Uig. The Morrisons used the broch as their stronghold, and impregnable it proved to be until Donald Cam Macaulay climbed up the outer face using two dirks as movable footholds or climbing-irons and smothered the Morrisons by throwing burning heather over them.

Scotland is not alone in possessing impressive prehistoric towers; Sardinia is thought to have as many as 6,500 stone-built *nuraghi*. The majority, however, were single-storeyed round-houses with corbelled roofs and it is only the most developed examples, dating to just before the late sixth century BC, that have a superficial similarity to Scottish brochs. In 1883 Joseph Anderson summed up the differences between the two traditions: 'No Broch has vaulted chambers disposed vertically over each other in the centre of the tower, and no Nuraghe has its centre open, and its chambers, stairs, and galleries arranged in the ring of walling surrounding the central court and windows looking into it as the Brochs have.' Radiocarbon dates now show that *nuraghi* probably began about 1400 BC, with the most sophisticated dating to 950-500 BC, thus being earlier than the development of the broch. Both forms of architecture are independent local evolutions at quite different periods.

9
Select gazetteer

Many brochs are pinpointed on Ordnance Survey maps; some are unmistakable, but others appear today as large masses of rubble with only a few diagnostic features to betray their original state.

Only the better preserved examples have been briefly listed here. The letters HS indicate that the monument is cared for by Historic Scotland on behalf of the Secretary of State for Scotland. At other sites the permission of the owner should be sought before entering private land. The sites are listed alphabetically within administrative councils and the National Grid Reference is given.

ARGYLL AND BUTE
Dun Mor Vaul, Tiree (OS 46: NM 042492). 2³/4 miles (4.5 km) north of Scarinish.

This is a well preserved broch with a carefully excavated collection of small finds (now in the Hunterian Museum, University of Glasgow). See chapter 6 and figures 21 and 22.

Tirefour, Lismore (OS 49: NM 867429). 1¹/2 miles (2.5 km) north-east of Achnacriosh.

This magnificent broch (figure 28) is in a beautiful setting. It has a solid-based wall with a distinct scarcement.

DUMFRIES AND GALLOWAY
Ardwell, Wigtown (OS 82: NX 067446). 10 miles (16 km) south of Stranraer.

This is the best preserved of the small group of brochs in south-west Scotland; there are two entrances, both with door-checks.

HIGHLAND
Caisteal Grugaig, Lochalsh (OS 33: NG 866250). Forestry Commission. 5¹/2 miles (9 km) north-west of Shiel Bridge.

The entrance is dominated by a massive triangular lintel. The passage, galleries and staircase may all be seen. See figure 24.

Carn Liath, Sutherland (OS 17: NC 870013). HS. South of A9, 2¹/2 miles (4 km) north-east of Golspie.

An accessible broch, the entrance and staircase remain visible; the inner wall-face is partly masked by a secondary building. See figure 25.

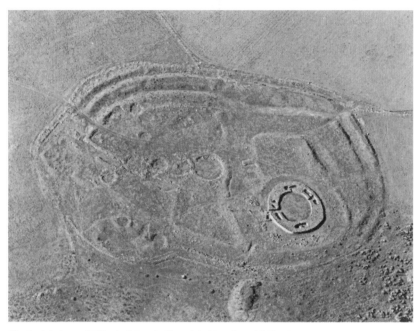

23. Aerial view of Edinshall broch, Berwickshire, Scottish Borders.

24. Caisteal Grugaig, Lochalsh, Highland: the inner end of the entrance passage.

Dun Ardtreck, Skye (OS 32: NG 335358). 3¹/2 miles (5.5 km) north-west of Carbost.

Situated dramatically on the edge of a cliff, this semibroch encloses an area about 13 by 10 metres (42 feet 6 inches by 30 feet). The entrance and basal gallery have been cleared of rubble in the course of excavation. See chapter 6 and figure 19.

Dun Beag, Struanmore, Skye (OS 32: NG 339386). HS. About ¹/2 mile (0.8 km) west of Bracadale.

The stonework is of high quality; the entrance passage, beehive cell, mural gallery and staircase are all well preserved. See figure 26.

Dun Borrafiach, Skye (OS 23: NG 235637). 5 miles (8 km) north-west of Lusta on the Waternish peninsula.

Dun Dornaigil, Sutherland (OS 9: NC 457450). HS. 1¹/4 miles (2 km) north-east of Eribol on the east side of the loch.

This impressive broch has a massive triangular lintel over the entrance. See figure 27.

Dun Fiadhairt, Skye (OS 23: NG 231504). 2¹/4 miles (3.5 km) north-west of Dunvegan.

Dun Hallin, Skye (OS 23: NG 256592). East of Hallin on the Waternish peninsula.

Dun Telve, Glenelg, Lochalsh (OS 33: NG 829172). HS. 1¹/2 miles (2.5 km) south-east of Glenelg.

Dun Telve is discussed in detail in chapter 2 and illustrated in figures 2-5.

Dun Troddan, Glenelg, Lochalsh (OS 33: NG 883172). HS. 1³/4 miles (3 km) south-east of Glenelg.

The broch still stands to a height of 8.5 metres (27 feet 10 inches). Excavations in the interior in 1920 revealed a ring of post-holes by which internal buildings were supported.

Ousdale, Caithness (OS 17: ND 071188). 3¹/2 miles (5.5 km) north-east of Helmsdale.

This broch is of particular interest as the entrance passage possesses two sets of door-checks; there is also a guard-cell and mural stair.

25. Carn Liath, Sutherland, Highland.

26. Dun Beag, Skye, Highland: drawn by Moses Griffith in 1772.

27. Dun Dornaigil, Sutherland, Highland.

ORKNEY
Borroughston, Shapinsay (OS 6: HY 540210). Near the north-east tip of the island.

The base of the broch is largely intact with a scarcement at a height of some 3 metres (10 feet); it has been protected by an outer rampart.

Borwick (OS 6: HY 224167). 5 miles (8 km) south-west of Dounby.

The broch occupies a position of considerable natural strength; the eastern half of the broch and the entrance passage are well preserved, but the western half has been destroyed by erosion.

Burrian, North Ronaldsay (OS 5: HY 762513). On the southern tip of the island.

This is a solid-based broch with entrance passage and cell; excavations in 1870-1 revealed a large collection of objects, now in the Royal Museum of Scotland, indicating iron age, Pictish and Early Christian activity.

Gurness, Mainland (OS 6: HY 381268). HS. On the promontory of Aikerness. 1^1/4 miles (2 km) north-east of Evie.
  This broch is discussed in chapter 5 and see figure 17. There is an informative site museum.

Midhowe, Rousay (OS 6: HY 371306). HS. 4^1/4 miles (7 km) north-west of Trumland.
  Midhowe is discussed in chapter 3.

SHETLAND
Burra Ness, Yell (OS 1: HU 557957). 2^1/4 miles (3.5 km) south of Gutcher.
  The broch still stands in part to a height of 3 metres (10 feet) and is additionally protected by twin outer ramparts.

Clickhimin (OS 4: HU 464408). HS. Just south-west of Lerwick.
  The broch is discussed in detail in chapter 4 and illustrated in figures 6 and 14.

Clumlie (OS 4: HU 404181). 5 miles (8 km) north of Sumburgh Airport.
  The broch is at the centre of a deserted croft; the broch wall, in which cells may still be seen, is over 2 metres (6 feet 6 inches) high.

Culswick (OS 4: HU 253448). 3^1/2 miles (5.5 km) west of Easter Skeld.
  This is a spectacular broch with the outer end of the entrance passage surmounted by a massive triangular lintel.

Jarlshof (OS 4: HU 398095). HS. About ^{1}/2 mile (1 km) south-east of Sumburgh Airport.
  This broch is discussed in detail in chapter 4 and see figure 12. There is a well presented site museum.

Mousa (OS 4: HU 457236). HS.
  The broch here is discussed in detail in chapter 4 and shown in figures 15 and 16. Weather conditions permitting, the ferry leaves from Sand pier: check timetable locally in advance.

SCOTTISH BORDERS
Bow (OS 73: NT 461417). 2 miles (3 km) south of Stow.
  The outline of the wall enclosing an area some 9.5 metres (31 feet) in diameter can still be seen.

28. Tirefour, Lismore, Argyll and Bute.

Edinshall, Berwickshire (OS 67: NT 772603). HS. 4 miles (6.5 km) north of Duns.

This is one of the best preserved of the southern brochs, set within an earlier fort and later settlement (figure 23). The entrance passage, guard-chambers and mural cells are clearly visible. The interior is unusually large – 17 metres (55 feet 9 inches) in diameter.

STIRLING

Coldoch (OS 57: NS 696981). 2³/4 miles (4.5 km) south-west of Doune.

Still standing to a height of 2.4 metres (7 feet 10 inches) the broch is about 9 metres (30 feet) in internal diameter; there are three cells and a staircase.

WESTERN ISLES

Dun an Sticir, North Uist (OS 18: NF 897776). Just south of Newtonferry.

Dun Baravat, Great Bernera, Lewis (OS 13: NB 155355). On the east side of the loch 1 mile (1.6 km) north-west of Barraglom.

On a small island, this broch has traces of a scarcement and an intra-mural gallery.

Dun Carloway, Lewis (OS 8 and 13: NB 190412). HS. 1¹/4 miles (2 km) south-west of Carloway.

See figure 20.

10
Museums

Intending visitors are advised to find out the times of opening before making a special journey.

Hunterian Museum, University of Glasgow, Glasgow G12 8QQ. Telephone: 0141-339 8855. Full displays of the finds from Dun Mor Vaul, Tiree; Dun Ardtreck, Skye; and Dun an Ruigh Ruaidh, Wester Ross.
Northlands Viking Centre, Auckengill, Caithness, Highland. Telephone: 01955 607702. Information about brochs in Caithness, particularly those excavated by Sir Francis Tress-Barry.
Royal Museum of Scotland, Chambers Street, Edinburgh EH1 1JF. Telephone: 0131-225 7534. The majority of finds from nineteenth- and twentieth-century excavations.
Shetland Museum, Lower Hillhead, Lerwick, Shetland ZE1 0EL. Telephone: 01595 695057.
Tankerness House Museum, Broad Street, Kirkwall, Orkney KW15 1DH. Telephone: 01856 873191.

There are site museums in the care of Historic Scotland at Jarlshof and Gurness.

11
Further reading

Anderson, J. *Scotland in Pagan Times. The Iron Age*. David Douglas, 1883.

Armit, I. (editor). *Beyond the Brochs: Changing Perspectives on the Later Iron Age in Atlantic Scotland*. Edinburgh University Press, 1990.

Armit, I. *The Archaeology of Skye and the Western Isles*. Edinburgh University Press, 1996.

Armit, I. *Celtic Scotland*. Batsford/Historic Scotland, 1997.

Barrett, J.C. 'Aspects of the Iron Age in Atlantic Scotland. A Case Study in the Problems of Archaeological Interpretation', *Proceedings of the Society of Antiquaries of Scotland*, 111 (1981), 205-19.

Baxter, S.P., McCullagh, R.P.J., and MacSween, A. 'The Iron Age in Shetland: Excavations at Five Sites Threatened by Coastal Erosion', *Proceedings of the Society of Antiquaries of Scotland*, 125 (1995), 429-82.

Callander, J.G., and Grant, W.G. 'The Broch of Midhowe, Rousay, Orkney', *Proceedings of the Society of Antiquaries of Scotland*, 68 (1933-4), 444-516.

Childe, V.G. *The Prehistory of Scotland*. Kegan Paul, 1935.

Close-Brooks, J. *Exploring Scotland's Heritage: The Highlands*. HMSO, 1995.

Cunliffe, B. *Iron Age Communities in Britain*. Routledge & Kegan Paul, 1978.

Fairhurst, H. *Excavations at Crosskirk Broch, Caithness*. Society of Antiquaries of Scotland, 1984.

Feachem, R. *A Guide to Prehistoric Scotland*. Batsford, second edition 1977.

Fojut, N. 'Is Mousa a Broch?', *Proceedings of the Society of Antiquaries of Scotland*, 111 (1981), 220-8.

Fojut, N. 'Some Thoughts on the Shetland Iron Age', in B. Smith (editor), *Shetland Archaeology*, 46-84. The Shetland Times, 1985.

Fojut, N. *The Brochs of Gurness and Midhowe*. Historic Scotland, 1993.

Graham, A. 'Some Observations on the Brochs', *Proceedings of the Society of Antiquaries of Scotland*, 81 (1946-7), 48-99.

Hamilton, J.R.C. *Excavations at Jarlshof, Shetland*. HMSO, 1956.

Hamilton, J.R.C. *Excavations at Clickhimin, Shetland*. HMSO, 1968.

Hedges, J. W. 'The Broch Period', in C. Renfrew (editor), *The Prehistory of Orkney*. Edinburgh University Press, 1985.

Hedges, J.W. *Bu, Gurness and the Brochs of Orkney*. British

Archaeological Reports, 163-5, 1987.

Hunter, M. *The Stronghold.* Hamish Hamilton Children's Books, 1974; Pan Books, 1978.

Macinnes, L. 'Brochs and the Roman Occupation of Lowland Scotland', *Proceedings of the Society of Antiquaries of Scotland,* 114 (1984), 235-49.

MacKie, E.W. 'The Origin and Development of the Broch and Wheelhouse Building Cultures of the Scottish Iron Age', *Proceedings of the Prehistoric Society,* 31 (1965), 93-146.

MacKie, E.W. 'English Migrants and Scottish Brochs', *Glasgow Archaeological Journal,* 2 (1971), 39-71.

MacKie, E.W. *Dun Mor Vaul. An Iron Age Broch on Tiree.* Glasgow University Press, 1974.

MacKie, E.W. 'The Brochs of Scotland', in P.J. Fowler (editor), *Recent Work in Rural Archaeology.* Moonraker, 1975.

Martlew, R. 'The Typological Study of the Structures of the Scottish Broch', *Proceedings of the Society of Antiquaries of Scotland,* 112 (1982), 254-76.

Megaw, J.V.S., and Simpson, D.D.A. *Introduction to British Prehistory.* Leicester University Press, 1979.

Ritchie, A. *Exploring Scotland's Heritage: Orkney.* TSO, 1996.

Ritchie, A. *Exploring Scotland's Heritage: Shetland.* TSO, 1997.

Ritchie, G. (editor). *The Archaeology of Argyll.* Edinburgh University Press, 1997.

Ritchie, G. and A. *Scotland: Archaeology and Early History.* Edinburgh University Press, 1991.

Ritchie, G., and Harman, M. *Exploring Scotland's Heritage: Argyll and the Western Isles.* HMSO, 1996.

Rivet, A.L.F. (editor). *The Iron Age in Northern Britain.* Edinburgh University Press, 1966.

Scott, Sir L. 'The Problem of the Brochs', *Proceedings of the Prehistoric Society,* 13 (1947), 1-36.

Smith, B. (editor). *Howe: Four Millennia of Orkney Prehistory.* Society of Antiquaries of Scotland, 1994.

Index

Page numbers in italics refer to illustrations.